* Continue clapping thus to end of bar 38.

faberYoungVoices

The Camden Music Shop
DOTS

132 St. Pancras Way,
London NW1 9NB

Tel: 020-7482-5424
Fax: 020-7482-5434
E-mail: dot@dotsonline.co.uk
Web: www.dotsonline.co.uk

3

CARIBBEAN CALYPSOS

Ophelia letter blow 'way
Linstead Market
Brown gal in de ring

Arranged by Peter Gritton

faberYoungVoices

FABER **ff** MUSIC

Ophelia letter blow 'way

Trinidad: traditional

Linstead Market

Jamaica: traditional

* ackee = vegetables   † 'quatty': an insignificant amount of money

8

* dem tan = they are
† nyam gran = taste good

Brown gal in de ring

Trinidad and Tobago: traditional

* like mixed percussion – drum kit, maracas, shakers, *etc.*

© 1995 by Faber Music Ltd.

* glottalised grunt.
† omit notes within brackets if baritone line is used.

The new *Faber Young Voices* series is devised specifically to address the needs of young or newly-formed choirs looking for easy, yet rewarding new repertoire.

Each volume offers:

◆ A coherent group of pieces to help with concert planning

◆ Arrangements or original pieces for soprano and alto voices with a manageable piano accompaniment

◆ An *optional* third line with a narrow range for 'baritone' (newly-broken or unstable voices) or low alto

◆ Excellent value for money

The series aims to span the fullest possible range of repertoire - both traditional and popular new material from folksongs, spirituals and calypsos to show songs and Christmas favourites.

◆ Faber Young Voices – the choral series for young choirs!

The Faber Young Voices Series:

Broadway Classics *arranged by Gwyn Arch* ISBN 0-571-51660-2
Christmas Fare *Jane Sebba* ISBN 0-571-51693-9
Classic Pop Ballads *arranged by Gwyn Arch* ISBN 0-571-51639-4
Favourites from Cats *Andrew Lloyd Webber* ISBN 0-571-51614-9
Folksongs from the Wild West *arranged by Gwyn Arch* ISBN 0-571-51533-9
Four Jazz Spirituals *arranged by Gwyn Arch* ISBN 0-571-51523-1
Get on Board! *arranged by Gwyn Arch* ISBN 0-571-51609-2
The Girl from Ipanema *arranged by Gwyn Arch* ISBN 0-571-51850-8
Gospel Rock *arranged by Gwyn Arch* ISBN 0-571-51638-6
Hits from 'Oklahoma' & 'The King & I' *Rodgers & Hammerstein* ISBN 0-571-51745-5
Hits from 'South Pacific' & 'Carousel' *Rodgers & Hammerstein* ISBN 0-571-51746-3
Metropolis *Lin Marsh* ISBN 0-571-52016-2
Pat-a-Pan *arranged by Gwyn Arch* ISBN 0-571-51691-2
Smash Hits for Christmas! *arranged by Gwyn Arch & Robert Winter* ISBN 0-571-51692-0
Songs of the City *arranged by Gwyn Arch* ISBN 0-571-51799-4
Three Caribbean Calypsos *arranged by Peter Gritton* ISBN 0-571-51527-4
Tropical Daydreams *Jane Sebba* ISBN 0-571-51865-6
Walking in the Air & other seasonal songs *Howard Blake* ISBN 0-571-58047-5
West End Showstoppers *arranged by Gwyn Arch* ISBN 0-571-51679-3

FABER MUSIC · 3 QUEEN SQUARE · LONDON   www.fabermusic.com

ISBN 0-571-51527-4

9 780571 515271